There are over 1,000 species of freshwater fishes in North America; this guide is intended to help novices identify a few of the most common, widespread and most heavily stocked fishes found here. With refinements in aquaculture, the most popular game fishes – including largemouth and smallmouth bass, trout and salmon, bluegill, crappies, and catfish – are now stocked in rivers, ponds and lakes throughout the U.S. and Canada.

Before Heading Out

To enjoy the fishing opportunities in your local lakes, ponds, waterways and reservoirs, you need to follow a few simple rules:

1. Purchase a fishing license if needed (regulations vary by state). Also purchase necessary tags to take specific species if needed.
2. Ensure it is legal to fish your location and that you are using legal baits and approved fishing procedures.
3. Be aware of minimum size and bag limits for each species you keep.

PARTS OF A BASS

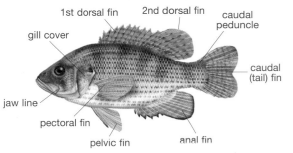

1st dorsal fin
2nd dorsal fin
caudal peduncle
gill cover
caudal (tail) fin
jaw line
pectoral fin
pelvic fin
anal fin

PARTS OF A TROUT

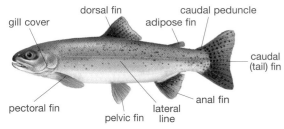

dorsal fin
caudal peduncle
adipose fin
gill cover
caudal (tail) fin
pectoral fin
pelvic fin
anal fin
lateral line

Most illustrations show the adult male in breeding coloration. Colors and markings may be duller or absent during different seasons. The measurements denote the approximate maximum length of species. Illustrations are not to scale.

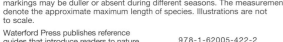

978-1-62005-422-2 $7.95 U.S.

BASS & FRESHWATER GAME FISH – An Illustrated Folding Pocket Guide to Familiar Species

Kavanagh/Leung

BASS & FRESHWATER GAME FISH

of North America

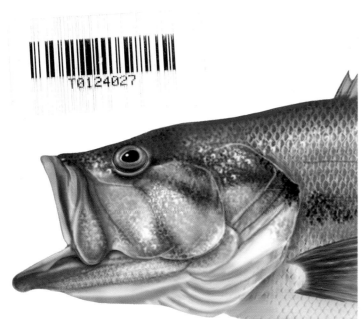

T012402T

An Illustrated Folding Pocket Guide to Familiar Species

Bass, sunfish and their allies all belong to the Order Perciformes. Most have a double dorsal fin; the 1st dorsal fin has spiny rays and the 2nd dorsal fin has soft rays.

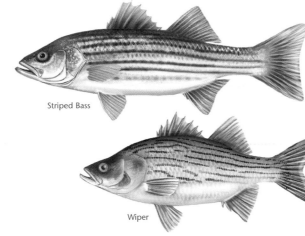

Striped Bass

Wiper

Striped Bass *Morone saxatilis*
Description: Has 6-9 dark side stripes on silvery sides. **Length:** To 6 ft. (1.8 m) **Weight:** To 69.5 lbs. (31.5 kg) **Habitat:** Coastal waters, some landlocked populations. **Range:** Native to Atlantic and Gulf coasts, it has been widely introduced to rivers and lakes. **Comments:** Hybrids with white bass – called 'wipers' or 'sunshine bass' – are similar but have deeper bodies, broken side stripes and are smaller (to 20 in./50 cm).

White Bass *Morone chrysops*
Description: Deep-bodied fish lacks side stripes. **Length:** To 18 in. (45 cm) **Weight:** To 7 lbs. (3 kg) **Habitat:** Large streams, rivers, lakes and reservoirs. **Range:** MB and the Great Lakes south to NM and MS. Widely introduced.

White Perch *Morone americana*
Description: Deep-bodied fish lacks side stripes. Head is depressed between the eyes and body is deepest under 1st dorsal fin. **Length:** To 22 in. (55 cm) **Weight:** To 3 lbs. (1.4 kg) **Habitat:** Brackish bays and estuaries, rivers and lakes. **Range:** Great Lakes and NS, south to SC, introduced elsewhere. **Comments:** Despite its common name, it is actually a bass.

Yellow Bass *Morone mississippiensis*
Description: Silvery-yellow fish has 5-9 black stripes on sides that are broken and offset below the lateral line. **Length:** To 18 in. (45 cm) **Weight:** To 2.7 lbs. (1.1 kg) **Habitat:** Quiet streams, lakes, backwaters and rivers. **Range:** MN and WI south to TX and AL. Introduced elsewhere. **Comments:** A prized sport and food fish.

Largemouth Bass *Micropterus salmoides*
Description: Dark olive to green fish has a dark mid-lateral stripe, often blotched. Has a very large mouth with the jaw line extending beyond the eye. **Length:** To 38 in. (95 cm) **Weight:** To 22.3 lbs. (10 kg) **Habitat:** Well vegetated lakes, ponds, streams. **Range:** Native to the Mississippi drainages and the deep south. **Comments:** The most sought-after North American game fish.

Smallmouth Bass *Micropterus dolomieu*
Description: Dark olive to brown fish has yellow-green sides and diffuse dark bars on sides. Jaw joint does not extend beyond the eye. **Length:** To 27 in. (68 cm) **Weight:** To 12 lbs. (5.4 kg) **Habitat:** Clear cool streams and rivers, shallow water of lakes. **Range:** Native to the Mississippi and Great Lakes drainages. **Comments:** Very popular game fish is widely stocked.

Spotted Bass *Micropterus punctulatus*
Description: Dark olive above, it has diamond-shaped mid-lateral blotches. Similar to the smallmouth bass, its jaw line does not extend beyond the eye and has rows of small black spots below the lateral line. **Length:** To 2 ft. (60 cm) **Weight:** To 10.4 lbs. (4.7 kg) **Habitat:** Warm waters. **Range:** WV and OH south to TX and FL. **Comments:** A prized sport fish that has been widely introduced.

Redear Sunfish
Lepomis microlophus
Description: Has orange or red spot near dark ear flap. **Length:** To 14 in. (35 cm) **Weight:** To 5.7 lbs. (2.6 kg) **Habitat:** Clear, quiet ponds, lakes and streams. **Range:** Southeastern U.S. Widely introduced. **Comments:** Also called shellcracker.

Green Sunfish
Lepomis cyanellus
Description: Has large mouth and dark spot on rear of second dorsal and anal fin. **Length:** To 12 in. (30 cm) **Weight:** To 4 lbs. (1.8 kg) **Habitat:** Clear ponds and streams with little current. **Range:** Widely introduced throughout the U.S. **Comments:** Tolerant of turbid water, it is very common and widespread.

Bluegill
Lepomis macrochirus
Description: Dark olive fish has brassy reflections. Ear flap is black. Note dark spot at the rear of the soft dorsal fin. **Length:** To 16 in. (40 cm) **Weight:** To 4.7 lbs. (2.2 kg) **Habitat:** Quiet, well-vegetated streams, ponds and lakes. **Range:** Widely introduced. **Comments:** One of the most popular game fish, it is very common throughout the eastern U.S. and Canada.

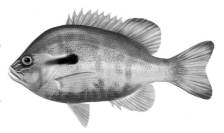

Redbreast Sunfish
Lepomis auritus
Description: Note bright orange breast, long ear flap and blue lines on cheek. **Length:** To 11 in. (28 cm) **Weight:** To 1.7 lbs. (.8 kg) **Habitat:** Streams, rivers, ponds and lakes. **Range:** Native to east coast. Widely introduced. **Comments:** Most common in streams.

Pumpkinseed
Lepomis gibbosus
Description: Green-orange fish has red-black spot on its ear flap. **Length:** To 16 in. (40 cm) **Weight:** To 1 lb. (.6 kg) **Habitat:** Warm, quiet, densely vegetated waters. **Range:** Native to eastern U.S. Widely introduced. **Comments:** Small, aggressive fish is often caught by novices.

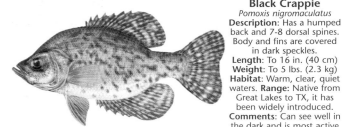

Black Crappie
Pomoxis nigromaculatus
Description: Has a humped back and 7-8 dorsal spines. Body and fins are covered in dark speckles. **Length:** To 16 in. (40 cm) **Weight:** To 5 lbs. (2.3 kg) **Habitat:** Warm, clear, quiet waters. **Range:** Native from Great Lakes to TX, it has been widely introduced. **Comments:** Can see well in the dark and is most active feeding in the evening.

White Crappie
Pomoxis annularis
Description: Has a humped back, 6 dorsal spines and 6-9 dark side blotches. **Length:** To 20 in. (50 cm) **Weight:** To 5.3 lbs. (2.4 kg) **Habitat:** Sandy or muddy bottomed streams and ponds, often in turbid water. **Range:** Native from Great Lakes to TX, it has been widely introduced. **Comments:** Is more tolerant of turbid water than the black crappie.

Warmouth
Lepomis gulosus
Description: Dark lines radiate back from red eye. **Length:** To 12 in. (30 cm) **Weight:** To 2.5 lbs. (1.1 kg) **Habitat:** Quiet water in vegetated lakes, ponds and swamps. **Range:** Introduced throughout U.S. **Comments:** Feeds under the cover of dense vegetation.

Longear Sunfish
Lepomis megalotis
Description: Olive to bluish fish has a yellow-orange belly and bluish lines on its face. Note long ear flap. **Length:** To 9 in. (23 cm) **Weight:** To 1.7 lbs. (.8 kg) **Habitat:** Densely vegetated streams, lakes, and reservoirs. **Range:** Eastern U.S. Widely introduced. **Comments:** Primarily a carnivore, it feeds on insects, snails and fishes.

Rock Bass
Ambloplites rupestris
Description: Robust olive to brown fish has blotched sides and red eyes. **Length:** To 17 in. (43 cm) **Weight:** To 3 lbs. (1.5 kg) **Habitat:** Cool, weedy lakes and streams over rocky bottoms. **Range:** Native to eastern U.S. Widely introduced. **Comments:** Also called black perch, rock sunfish.

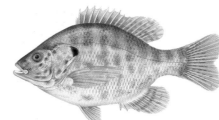

PERCH & ALLIES

Yellow Perch *Perca flavescens*
Description: Deep-bodied, green to yellowish fish has 6-9 dark 'saddles' down its side. **Length**: To 16 in. (40 cm) **Weight**: To 4 lbs. (1.9 kg) **Habitat**: Clear, vegetated streams and lakes. **Range**: Native to northern and eastern North America; widely introduced in some areas.

Walleye *Sander vitreus*
Description: Olive green fish has sides covered with gold flecks. Note dark blotch on rear of first dorsal fin and a white tip on the lower lobe of its caudal fin. **Length**: To 40 in. (1 m) **Weight**: To 25 lbs. (11 kg) **Habitat**: Clear, clear, streams and creeks, often in turbid waters. **Range**: Most of Canada, south to Mississippi and Gulf coast drainages. Widely introduced. **Comments**: One of the most sought after food fish.

Sauger *Sander canadensis*
Description: Cylindrical, has 3-4 dark saddles on sides. Note black crescents on first dorsal fin. **Length**: To 30 in. (75 cm) **Weight**: To 8.7 lbs. (4 kg) **Habitat**: Large rivers and creeks, often in turbid waters. **Range**: Southern Canada from AB to QC, south to LA and west of the Appalachians. Widely introduced. **Comments**: An important sport fish, it is harvested commercially in Canada.

PIKE & ALLIES

Northern Pike *Esox lucius*
Description: Note large head and posterior dorsal fin. Sides are covered with rows of light, bean-shaped spots. **Length**: To 53 in. (1.4 m) **Weight**: To 55 lbs. (25 kg) **Habitat**: Slow-moving streams and lakes with abundant vegetation. **Range**: Alaska and northern Canada south to NE and PA; widely introduced. **Comments**: Also called jackfish, it is the most widely distributed North American fish.

PIKE & ALLIES

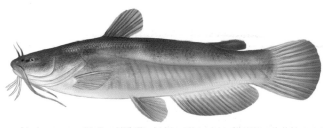

Muskellunge *Esox masquinongy*
Description: Huge, torpedo-shaped fish has dark blotches on its back. **Length**: To 6 ft. (1.8 m) **Weight**: To 67.5 lbs. (30 kg) **Habitat**: Lakes, rivers and large reservoirs with abundant vegetation. **Range**: The Great Lakes region south to KY; widely introduced. **Comments**: A prized sport fish, the 'muskie' will eat anything it can swallow including amphibians, birds and small mammals.

Chain Pickerel *Esox niger*
Description: Olive/brown to yellowish fish has a chain-like pattern on sides. **Length**: To 31 in. (78 cm) **Weight**: To 9.4 lbs. (4 kg) **Habitat**: Clear, well-vegetated lakes, ponds and swamps. **Range**: Eastern coastal waters from QC to FL and Mississippi River systems. **Comments**: Popular ice-fishing species in winter.

CATFISH

Catfish have sensitive barbels (whiskers) that they use to locate food. Most catfish have a spine-like ray on the leading edge of the dorsal and pectoral fins. Caution should be taken when landing these fish.

Blue Catfish *Ictalurus furcatus*
Description: Note straight-edged anal fin. Body lacks dark spots. **Length**: To 5.5 ft. (1.7 m) **Weight**: To 143 lbs. (65 kg) **Habitat**: Large, clear rivers and lakes over rocky or sandy soils. **Range**: Mississippi River system from SD and WV, south to GA and TX; widely introduced. **Comments**: One of the largest North American freshwater fishes.

Channel Catfish *Ictalurus punctatus*
Description: Note black-spotted sides and rounded anal fin. Upper lobe of caudal fin is white. **Length**: To 4 ft. (1.2 m) **Weight**: To 58 lbs. (26 kg) **Habitat**: Large, slow-moving streams and rivers. **Range**: AB to QC, south throughout central and east-central U.S. **Comments**: A popular sport and food fish, it has been widely introduced outside of its native range and is often used in aquaculture.

CATFISH

Yellow Bullhead *Ameiurus natalis*
Description: Olive to brown above, it has a yellowish belly and sides. Chin barbels are white or yellow. Anal and caudal fin are white-tipped. **Length**: To 18 in. (45 cm) **Weight**: To 6.4 lbs. (2.9 kg) **Habitat**: Sluggish streams, pools and backwaters. **Range**: Native to Atlantic drainages, it has been widely introduced. **Comments**: A good food and sport fish, it is active primarily at night.

Black Bullhead *Ameiurus melas*
Description: Back is olive to black, sides and belly are yellowish. Chin barbels (whiskers) are black. Anal fin is relatively short. **Length**: To 2 ft. (60 cm) **Weight**: To 8 lbs. (3.7 kg) **Habitat**: Pools and sluggish streams, often over soft soils. **Range**: Great Lakes region to MB, south to TX and MS. **Comments**: More tolerant of silty water than other bullheads.

Brown Bullhead *Ameiurus nebulosus*
Description: Brown above, white below with mottled sides. **Length**: To 19 in. (48 cm) **Weight**: To 7.4 lbs. (3.3 kg) **Habitat**: Clear, deep water with abundant vegetation. **Range**: SK south to LA, east to Atlantic coast. **Comments**: Raised commercially in many areas.

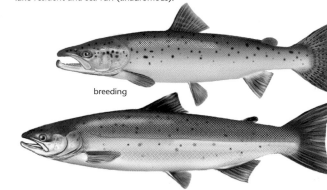

Flathead Catfish *Pylodictis olivaris*
Description: Brown to olive fish has a large, wide, flat head. Upper lobe of caudal fin is white. **Length**: To 5 ft. (1.5 m) **Weight**: To 123 lbs. (56 kg) **Habitat**: Large creeks, rivers and reservoirs. **Range**: Central U.S. east to PA and south to AL, LA and TX. **Comments**: An important sport and food fish.

TROUT & ALLIES

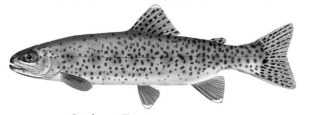

steelhead breeding coloration

Rainbow Trout *Oncorhynchus mykiss*
Description: Body and fins are dark-spotted. Coloration is highly variable, ranging from steely blue, to yellow-green, to brown. Pink to red side stripe is most vivid in males during breeding season. Rainbow trout that go to sea are called steelhead, these fish spend 2-3 years at sea before returning to freshwater to spawn. **Length**: To 44 in. (1.1 m) **Weight**: To 48 lbs. (22 kg) **Habitat**: Large rivers, lakes and freshwater streams. **Range**: Native to western North America, it has been widely introduced throughout the world. **Comments**: A popular food fish, it is one of the most common farmed fish.

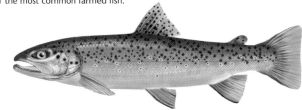

Brown Trout *Salmo trutta*
Description: Olive to brown above, it is covered with red, black or orange spots, often with white halos. Caudal fin is straight-edged. Interior of mouth is all-white. **Length**: To 40 in. (1 m) **Weight**: To 42 lbs. (19 kg) **Habitat**: Cool, fast-flowing streams and lakes. Some sea-run populations occur in nearshore waters. **Range**: Native to Europe, widely stocked throughout the U.S. and Canada. **Comments**: Like rainbow and cutthroat trout, there are three basic forms, stream-resident, lake-resident and sea-run (anadromous).

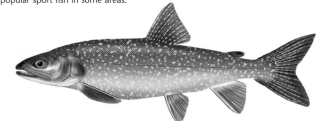

breeding

Atlantic Salmon *Salmo salar*
Description: Silvery-blue fish has black spots (often X-shaped) on sides (but not on fins) and 2-3 large spots on gill cover. Interior of mouth is all-white. Breeding form is brown-purple on sides and has red spots and a hooked lower jaw. Both anadromous and landlocked forms occur. **Length**: To 4.5 ft. (1.4 m) **Weight**: To 26.7 lbs. (12 kg) **Habitat**: Coastal waters, freshwater lakes and streams. **Range**: Native from Arctic Circle through N Quebec to Connecticut River and Europe. Many populations are threatened with extinction. **Comments**: Widely stocked in freshwater lakes.

TROUT & ALLIES

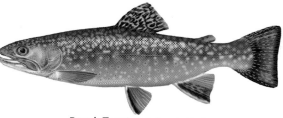

Cutthroat Trout *Oncorhynchus clarkii*
Description: Has a reddish mark under lower jaw. Color is highly variable, ranging from olive to bluish to red. Has a dark-spotted body and upper fins but lacks spots on top of head. **Length**: To 39 in. (99 cm) **Weight**: To 41 lbs. (18 kg) **Habitat**: Small streams and lakes. **Range**: Native to Pacific coast, Rocky Mountain and Great Basin drainages. **Comments**: 14 subspecies are native to distinct regions.

Brook Trout *Salvelinus fontinalis*
Description: Has wavy yellow marks on dorsal side and dorsal fin. Pelvic, pectoral and anal fins have a white leading edge. Reddish side spots have blue halos. The breeding male is brilliant red-orange below and has a black belly. **Length**: To 28 in. (70 cm) **Weight**: To 14 lbs. (6.4 kg) **Habitat**: Cool, clean rivers and lakes. **Range**: Native to Eastern Canada and the Great Lakes south to GA, introduced elsewhere. **Comments**: Hybrids of brook and lake trout – called splake – are a popular sport fish in some areas.

breeding

Lake Trout *Salvelinus namaycush*
Description: Blue-gray to olive above, its body is covered in pale, often bean-shaped, spots. Pelvic, pectoral and anal fins are often red-orange with a white leading edge. Caudal fin is deeply forked. Individuals inhabiting large lakes may be silvery overall. **Length**: To 50 in. (1.3 m) **Weight**: To 72 lbs. (33 kg) **Habitat**: Deep, cold lakes and rivers. **Range**: AK and most of Canada south to the Great Lakes, introduced elsewhere. **Comments**: The largest North American trout is a prized food fish.

Chinook Salmon *Oncorhynchus tshawytscha*
Description: Has silvery sides and black spots on its upper body. Gums are black at tooth base. **Length**: To 5 ft. (1.5 m) **Weight**: To 46 lbs. (20.8 kg) **Habitat**: Large rivers and lakes. **Range**: Widely introduced. **Comments**: Chinook salmon were introduced to the Great Lakes in 1967 and still thrive there.

TROUT & ALLIES

breeding

Kokanee Salmon *Oncorhynchus nerka*
Description: Landlocked sockeye salmon has a silvery body and bluish back. Red breeding male has hooked jaws and a green head. **Length**: To 18 in. (46 cm) **Weight**: To 9.6 lbs. (4.3 kg) **Habitat**: Large lakes. **Range**: Bering Strait to central CA. **Comments**: Does not migrate and may be found in the same lakes as its sea-run relatives.

Lake Whitefish *Coregonus clupeaformis*
Description: Distinguished by their compressed body, subterminal mouth and forked caudal fin. Brown to blue above, sides are silvery. Note concave overall. **Length**: To 30 in. (75 cm) **Weight**: To 15 lbs. (6.8 kg) **Habitat**: Large rivers and lakes. **Range**: Throughout much of Canada, south to the Great Lakes. **Comments**: Primarily a bottom-feeder, it is a valued food fish and is one of the most valuable commercial fish in North America.